AAT

Drafting and Interpreting Financial Statements

Pocket Notes

These Pocket Notes support study for the following AAT qualifications:
AAT Professional Diploma in Accounting – Level 4
AAT Diploma in Business Skills – Level 4
AAT Diploma in Professional Accounting at SCQF Level 8

British library cataloguing-in-publication data

A catalogue record for this book is available from the British Library.

Published by:
Kaplan Publishing UK
Unit 2 The Business Centre
Molly Millars Lane
Wokingham
Berkshire
RG41 2QZ

ISBN 978-1-83996-910-2

© Kaplan Financial Limited, 2024

Printed and bound in Great Britain.

The text in this material and any others made available by any Kaplan Group company does not amount to advice on a particular matter and should not be taken as such. No reliance should be placed on the content as the basis for any investment or other decision or in connection with any advice given to third parties. Please consult your appropriate professional adviser as necessary. Kaplan Publishing Limited, all other Kaplan group companies, the International Accounting Standards Board, and the IFRS Foundation expressly disclaim all liability to any person in respect of any losses or other claims, whether direct, indirect, incidental, consequential or otherwise arising in relation to the use of such materials. Printed and bound in Great Britain.

Acknowledgements

This product contains copyright material and trademarks of the IFRS Foundation®. All rights reserved. Used under licence from the IFRS Foundation®. Reproduction and use rights are strictly limited. For more information about the IFRS Foundation and rights to use its material please visit HYPERLINK "http://www.ifrs.org" www.ifrs.org.

Disclaimer: To the extent permitted by applicable law the Board and the IFRS Foundation expressly disclaims all liability howsoever arising from this publication or any translation thereof whether in contract, tort or otherwise (including, but not limited to, liability for any negligent act or omission) to any person in respect of any claims or losses of any nature including direct, indirect, incidental or consequential loss, punitive damages, penalties or costs.

Information contained in this publication does not constitute advice and should not be substituted for the services of an appropriately qualified professional.

The IFRS Foundation logo, the IASB logo, the IFRS for SMEs logo, the 'Hexagon Device', 'IFRS Foundation', 'eIFRS', 'IAS', 'IASB', 'IFRS for SMEs', 'IASs', 'IFRS', 'IFRSs', 'International Accounting Standards' and 'International Financial Reporting Standards', 'IFRIC', NIIF® and 'SIC' are Trade Marks of the IFRS Foundation.

Trade Marks

The Foundation has trade marks registered around the world ('Trade Marks') including 'IAS®', 'IASB®', 'IFRIC®', 'IFRS®', the IFRS® logo, 'IFRS for SMEs®', IFRS for SMEs® logo, the 'Hexagon Device', 'International Financial Reporting Standards®', NIIF® and 'SIC®'.

Further details of the Foundation's Trade Marks are available from the Licensor on request.

This product contains material that is ©Financial Reporting Council Ltd (FRC). Adapted and reproduced with the kind permission of the Financial Reporting Council. All rights reserved. For further information, please visit www.frc.org.uk or call +44 (0)20 7492 2300.

CONTENTS

		Study Text chapter	Page Number
A guide to the assessment			1
Chapter 1	The reporting frameworks and types of business organisation	1, 2	5
Chapter 2	Limited company financial statements	3, 12	15
Chapter 3	Tangible and intangible assets	4, 5, 6	31
Chapter 4	Key accounting standards	7, 8, 9, 10, 11	45
Chapter 5	Interpretation of financial statements	13	57
Chapter 6	Statement of cash flows	14	63
Chapter 7	Group accounts: basic principles and consolidated statement of financial position	15, 16	71
Chapter 8	Group accounts: consolidated statement of profit or loss	17	79
References			R 1
Index			I.1

This document references IFRS® Standards and IAS® Standards, which are authored by the International Accounting Standards Board (the Board), and published in the 2020 blue book.

Drafting and Interpreting Financial Statements

Preface

These Pocket Notes contain the key things that you need to know for the exam, presented in a unique visual way that makes revision easy and effective.

Written by experienced lecturers and authors, these Pocket Notes break down content into manageable chunks to maximise your concentration.

Quality and accuracy are of the utmost importance to us so if you spot an error in any of our products, please send an email to mykaplanreporting@kaplan.com with full details, or follow the link to the feedback form in MyKaplan.

Our Quality Co-ordinator will work with our technical team to verify the error and take action to ensure it is corrected in future editions.

A guide to the assessment

- Examinable International Financial Reporting Standards (both IFRS and IAS).

A guide to the assessment

The assessment

This unit is concerned with competence in drafting and interpreting the financial statements of limited companies.

Learners will have already attained competence at Levels 2 and 3 in the process of identifying and recording financial transactions in accounts and ledgers following the principles of double entry bookkeeping. They will already be able to draft the financial statements of sole traders and partnerships. This unit develops and applies these competencies further by focusing on the drafting and interpretation of financial statements of limited companies.

Learners are also introduced to tools and techniques that can be used to analyse and interpret the financial performance and financial position of a company.

Examination

Drafting and Interpreting Financial Statements (DAIF) is assessed by means of a computer based assessment (CBA). The CBA will last for two and a half hours and will consist of 7 tasks.

In any one assessment, learners may not be assessed on all content, or on the full depth or breadth of a piece of content. The content assessed may change over time to ensure validity of assessment, but all assessment criteria will be assessed over time.

A guide to the assessment

Learning outcomes and weighting

1. Understand the reporting frameworks that underpin financial reporting. 7%
2. Draft statutory financial statements for a limited company 43%
3. Draft consolidated financial statements 25%
4. Interpret financial statements using ratio analysis 25%

Total 100%

Pass mark

To pass a unit assessment, students need to achieve a mark of 70% or more.

This unit contributes 15% of the total amount required for the Professional Diploma in Accounting qualification.

Examinable International Financial Reporting Standards (both IFRS® Standards and IAS® Standards)

IAS 1	Presentation of Financial Statements
IAS 2	Inventories
IAS 7	Statement of Cash Flows
IAS 10	Events After the Reporting Period
IAS 12	Income Taxes
IAS 16	Property, Plant and Equipment
IAS 36	Impairment of Assets
IAS 37	Provisions, Contingent Liabilities and Contingent Assets
IAS 38	Intangible Assets
IFRS 3	Business Combinations
IFRS 10	Consolidated Financial Statements
IFRS 15	Revenue from Contracts with Customers
IFRS 16	Leases

chapter 1

The reporting frameworks and types of business organisation

- Overview.
- IFRS foundation.
- Legal framework.
- The framework.
- IAS 1 Presentation of Financial Statements.
- Different types of business organisation.
- Differences between preparing accounts for a sole trader and a limited company.
- Differences between a private and a public company.

The reporting frameworks and types of business organisation

Overview

This chapter gives information on:

- the regulatory environment (company law and the IFRS Foundation)
- the conceptual framework (the Conceptual Framework for Financial Reporting).

CBA focus

You may be required to discuss or explain topics in this chapter as part of an examination task.

IFRS foundation

The structure of the International Financial Reporting Standards Foundation (IFRS Foundation) and its subsidiary bodies is shown below:

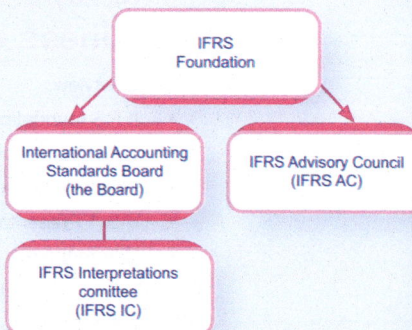

Key Point

- The IFRS Foundation is an independent not for profit foundation based in the US whose trustees appoint the members of the Board, IFRS AC and IFRS IC.
- The Board is responsible for developing and issuing new accounting standards. The Board issues International Financial Reporting Standards (IFRS® Standards) and has adopted the previous International Accounting Standards (IAS® Standards).
- The IFRS AC advises the Board on priorities in its work and informs the Board of the implications of proposed standards for users and preparers of financial statements.
- The IFRS IC draws up interpretations if a new problem arises or gives guidance on the application of a standard where unsatisfactory interpretations exist.

Legal framework

- In the UK, companies must prepare their financial statements following the rules laid out in the Companies Act 2006 (CA06).
- The CA06 has been amended to reflect the fact that some companies prepare their financial statements based upon the application of IFRS Standards.
- In the UK, the Financial Reporting Council (FRC) prepares accounting standards. In recent years there has been a process of harmonisation between UK and International standards and the majority of UK standards are now equivalent to IFRS Standards.

The framework

The Framework for Financial Reporting identifies the principles on which accounting standards are to be developed. It aims to assist in the preparation of financial statements, development of new standards and to reduce alternative accounting treatments.

Key Point

- The underlying assumption of financial statements is that they are prepared on a going concern basis.
- There are two fundamental qualitative characteristics together with four enhancing characteristics:

The two fundamental qualitative characteristics:

- **Relevance** – financial information is regarded as relevant if it capable of influencing the decision of users.
- **Faithful representation** – this means that financial information must be complete, neutral and free from error.

The four enhancing qualititative characteristics:

- **Comparability** – it should be possible to compare an entity over time and with similar information about other entities.
- **Verifiability** – if information can be verified (e.g. through an audit) this provides assurance to the users that it is both credible and reliable.
- **Timeliness** – information should be provided to users within a timescale suitable for their decision making purposes.
- **Understandability** – information should be understandable to those that might want to review and use it. This can be facilitated through appropriate classification, characterisation and presentation of information.

Elements of the financial statements

Asset: 'a present economic resource controlled by an entity as a result of a past event'.

Liability: 'a present obligation of the entity to transfer an economic resource as a result of a past event'.

Equity: 'the residual interest in the assets of the entity after deducting all its liabilities'.

Income: 'the increase in economic benefits during an accounting period'.

Expenses: 'the decrease in economic benefits during an accounting period'.

Recognition of items in the financial statements

Recognition of (i.e. recording) an item in the financial statements occurs if:

- the item meets the definition of an element
- it provides relevant information regarding the particular element
- it provides a faithful representation of the particular element

IAS 1 Presentation of Financial Statements

IAS 1 provides formats for the statement of profit or loss, statement of financial position and statement of changes in equity as well as setting out six accounting concepts that should be applied:

- **going concern** – the business will continue in operation for the foreseeable future
- **accruals** – the effects of transactions and other events are recognised as they occur and not as cash or its equivalent is received or paid
- **consistency of presentation** – items in the financial statements are presented and classified in the same way from one period to the next unless there is a change in the operations of the business or a new standard requires a change in presentation
- **materiality and aggregation** – each material class of similar items shall be presented separately in the financial statements
- **offsetting** – assets and liabilities and income and expenses cannot be offset unless a standard requires it
- **comparative information** – should be shown for all amounts reported in the financial statements.

Accounting policies should be selected so that the financial statements comply with all international standards and interpretations.

An entity must make an explicit statement in the notes to the financial statements that they comply with IFRS Standards.

Different types of business organisation

For profit organisations are businesses whose primary goal is making money (a profit).

Not-for-profit organisations are non-profit making. They are usually charities, clubs and societies.

Sole traders are businesses which are owned and run by one individual. The owner is responsible for any business debts.

Partnerships are businesses which are owned and run by two or more persons. The partners are responsible for any business debts.

Limited companies are classed as their own legal entity where the shareholders (investors) are the owners.

Limited liability partnerships (LLPs) are partnerships where some or all of the partners have limited liabilities similar to shareholders in a company.

Charities are organisations which meet the definition of a charity set out in the Charities Act 2011. It must be established for charitable purposes only, meaning that it must be for the general benefit of the public. It needs to be established for specific purposes for example the advancement of education, the advancement of religion and the advancement of arts and culture.

Public sector organisations are responsible for providing all Public Services in the UK. From Healthcare to Education, Social Care to Housing, Refuse Collection to International Development, Tourism Promotion to Pensions. Funding comes through taxation, collected locally and centrally and through revenue earning activities.

Differences between preparing accounts for a sole trader and a limited company

Legal requirements

There is no legal requirement for sole traders and partnerships to prepare accounts but they may find it useful to assess the financial performance and position of their business.

Limited companies have a legal requirement to prepare final accounts annually in line with the relevant accounting standards. If the company has adopted IFRSs then it must prepare accounts in the format outlined by International Accounting Standard 1 (IAS 1).

Tax

Sole traders and partners in a partnership pay income tax on their share of the taxable profits. Companies pay corporation tax on their taxable profits and this will be charged to the statement of profit or loss as an expense.

Borrowings

Sole traders and partners in a partnership are free to borrow from the business bank account how they wish, this is classed as drawings. If the business bank account runs to an overdraft then the owners are personally liable for the debts. Directors (only) in a company can sometimes withdraw cash from the company provided it is within the limits set out in Companies Act 2006.

Differences between a private and a public company

	Public companies	Private (limited) companies
Definition	Registered as a public company.	Any company that is not a public company.
Name	Ends with plc or public limited company.	Ends with ltd or limited.
Capital	Not less than the authorised minimum (currently £50,000).	No minimum requirements.
Raising capital	Can raise capital by selling shares to the public.	Prohibited from selling shares to the public.
Trading	Must obtain a trading certificate from Companies House before the commencement of trading.	Can start trading from the date of incorporation.
Shareholders	Minimum of two.	Minimum of one.
Directors	Minimum of two.	Minimum of one.
Accounts	Must file accounts at Companies House within six months of financial year-end.	Must file accounts at Companies House within nine months of financial year-end.
Audit	Accounts must be audited.	Audit not required if meets exemption criteria.

chapter 2

Limited company financial statements

- Overview.
- Features of limited companies.
- Contents of company financial statements.
- Company finance.
- Share issues.
- Dividends.
- Tax.

Limited company financial statements

Overview

- The chapter explains the main 'legal' features of limited liability companies which distinguish them from sole traders and partnerships.
- The information and statements making up the financial statements of a company are introduced, with particular emphasis on the 'Statement of changes in equity' – this statement is relevant only to companies.
- The main sources of company finance (equity and debt) are introduced together with an explanation of the items which may be encountered under each of these headings.
- The accounting treatment of the following are explained:
  - Share issues, including bonus and rights issues.
  - Dividends.
  - Taxation.

Features of limited companies

Companies are distinguished from other types of business by the following three factors:

1. The law regards a company as a **separate legal entity** from its shareholders.
2. The **separation of the ownership** (shareholders) **from the management** (directors) of the company.
3. The **limited liability** of shareholders for the debts of a company. Their liability is limited to any portion of the nominal value of shares that is unpaid.

Key points:

- The shareholders can share in the profits of the company without having to work in the business on a day-to-day basis.
- It is easy for a company to borrow money, as they are able to as they are able to raise loan finance by the issue of a debenture.
- If the shareholders die the company will not cease trading which would be the case with a sole trader.
- Companies may have to be audited and have to prepare their financial statements according to prescribed formats.
- There is more administration to deal with in a company such as filing financial statements with the Registrar of Companies.
- Companies are regulated by the Companies Act 2006 and accounting standards issued by the IASB.

Contents of company financial statements

A set of financial statements includes the following statements:

- Statement of financial position
- Statement of profit or loss
- Statement of changes in equity
- Statement of cash flows

The other parts of the financial statements are:

- **Accounting policy note** – to disclose the policies adopted by the company for items in the financial statements.
- **Notes to the financial statements** – to provide more detailed information about the figures included in the statement of financial position, statement of profit or loss and statement of cash flows.

- **Comparative figures** – to show the position in the previous financial year for comparison purposes.

Formats

The format of the statement of profit or loss and other comprehensive income is detailed in IAS 1 Presentation of Financial Statements and is shown below.

Statement of profit or loss and other comprehensive income	£
Continuing operations	
Revenue	X
Cost of sales	(X)
Gross profit	X
Distribution costs	(X)
Administrative expenses	(X)
Profit from operations	X
Finance costs	(X)
Profit before tax	X
Tax	(X)
Profit for the period from continuing operations	X
Other comprehensive income for the year	
Gain on revaluation of land	X
Total comprehensive income for year	X

The statement of financial position and principal notes to the accounts are shown below.

Company statement of financial position at 31 December 20XX

ASSETS	£000
Non-current assets	
Goodwill	X
Other intangible assets	X
Property, plant and equipment	X
Investments in subsidiaries	X
Investments in associates	X
Current assets	
Inventories	X
Trade and other receivables	X
Cash and cash equivalents	X
Total assets	X

EQUITY AND LIABILITIES

Equity
Share capital	X
Share premium account	X
Revaluation surplus	X
Retained earnings	X
Total equity	**X**

Non-current liabilities
Bank loans	X
Long-term provisions	X

Current liabilities
Trade and other payables	X
Tax liabilities	X
Bank overdrafts and loans	X
Total equity and liabilities	**X**

An example of a property, plant and equipment note is shown below:

	Land and buildings	Plant and machinery	Fixtures, fittings, and equipment	Total
	£000	£000	£000	£000
Cost or valuation:				
At 1 January 20XX	X	X	X	X
Additions	X	X	X	X
Disposals	–	(X)	(X)	(X)
At 31 December 20XX	X	X	X	X

Continued on next page:-

Limited company financial statements

	Land and buildings	Plant and machinery	Fixtures, fittings, tools and equipment	Total
	£000	£000	£000	£000
Accumulated depreciation:				
At 1 January 20XX	X	X	X	X
Charge for year	X	X	X	X
Disposals	–	(X)	(X)	(X)
At 31 December 20XX	X	X	X	X
Carrying amount:				
at 1 January 20XX	X	X	X	X
at 31 December 20XX	X	X	X	X

Statement of Changes in Equity

Below is a pro forma Statement of Changes in Equity:

	Share capital £000	Share premium £000	Revaluation surplus £000	Retained earnings £000	Total £000
At 1 January 20XX	X	X	X	X	X
Total comprehensive income for the year			X	X	X
Dividends paid				(X)	(X)
At 31 December 20XX	X	X	X	X	X

Limited company financial statements

Key points:

The statement of changes in equity:

- This statement shows all the gains and losses in the period including those which are not recognised in the statement of profit or loss such as revaluation surpluses.
- As the statement of profit or loss does not show dividends paid in the period, this is also shown in this statement.
- It is essentially a reconciliation of share capital and reserves from the opening to the closing position.

Company finance

The way companies are financed varies from one company to another. Typically, companies will have a combination of equity finance (from shareholders) and debt finance (from banks and other lenders).

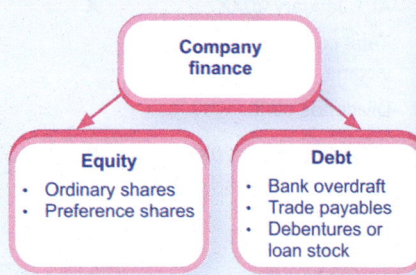

- **Ordinary shares** (or equity shares) give shareholders the right to vote at general meetings of the company and to receive dividends from profits.
- **Preference shares** carry a fixed rate of dividend but the shareholders are not given a vote. The preference dividend is paid in priority to the ordinary dividend.
- **Debentures or loan stock** are loans shown as liabilities in the statement of financial position. A debenture may be a loan from one person, whereas loan stock may be held by a number of individuals, like shares.
- These loans have interest charged which is an expense in the statement of profit or loss. The accounting entries are:

    DR Interest expense

    CR Accruals/cash (depending on whether the cash has actually been paid).

Share issues

Shares may be issued at their nominal (or par) value or at a premium (an amount in excess of their nominal value).

Example

A Ltd issued 1,000 ordinary shares with a nominal value of £1 for £1.20 cash.

The double entry to record this is:

	£	£
DR Cash (1,000 × £1.20)	1,200	
CR Share capital (nominal value = 1,000 × £1)		1,000
CR Share premium (1,000 × £0.2)		200

Bonus issues

Extra shares are issued to existing shareholders in proportion to their shareholding without any money being paid for them.

The accounting entries are:

DR Retained earnings (or any other reserve, such as revaluation surplus or share premium)

CR Share capital

This may be done to increase the number of shares so that the share price is reduced and the shares are more marketable.

Rights issues

Extra shares are issued at a favourable price to existing shareholders. The number of shares they can buy is in proportion to their existing shareholding, such as 1 share for every 5 they own – a 1 for 5 issue.

The accounting entries are the same as a normal share issue.

Example

A Ltd has 400,000 50p ordinary shares in issue and makes a rights issue of 100,000 50p ordinary shares at 90p per share. The issue is fully taken up.

Required:
Show the entries in the relevant ledger accounts.

Tutorial note
Rights issue: 100,000 × £0.50 = £50,000 is entered in the share capital account. 100,000 × £0.40 = £40,000 is entered in the share premium account.

Solution

Share capital

	£		£
Balance c/d	250,000	Balance b/f (400,000 × 0.5)	200,000
		Bank (100,000 × 0.5)	50,000
	250,000		250,000
		Balance b/d	250,000

Bank

	£		£
Share capital	50,000		
Share premium	40,000		
	90,000		

Share premium

	£		£
Balance c/d	40,000	Bank (100,000 × 0.4)	40,000
	40,000		40,000
		Balance b/d	40,000

Dividends

- Dividends are payments made to shareholders. They can be stated as an amount per share e.g. 5p per share dividend or on a percentage basis e.g. 5% on a £1 share.
- Both the interim and final dividends paid are shown in the notes to the financial statements. Any dividends declared before the year end are included in payables. The double entry bookkeeping for dividends is as follows:

Interim dividend paid:

Dr Retained Earnings

Cr Cash

Final dividend payable:

Dr Retained Earnings

Cr Payables

Tax

- Companies must pay tax on their profits.
- At the year-end, the tax is estimated and charged in the statement of profit or loss.
- In the UK corporation tax is paid nine months after the year-end so the amount provided might not be the actual amount paid.
- When the tax is estimated, the accounting entries are:

    DR Tax expense (SPL)
    CR Tax payable (SFP)

- When the tax is paid, the accounting entries are:

    DR Tax payable (SFP)
    CR Cash (SFP)

- Any under or overprovision of tax must be adjusted in the following year's financial statements.
    - If the company provided for too much tax then there will be a credit in the following year's tax charge.
    - If the company didn't provide enough tax then the following year will have an additional charge of the shortfall.

Example

For the year ended 30 September 20X7, the estimated tax charge was £30,000.

For the year ended 30 September 20X8, the estimated tax charge was £40,000, and the actual tax paid for the previous year was £32,000.

Show these entries in the tax expense accounts for the two years.

Solution

Taxation expense

	£		£
20X7			
Tax liability a/c	30,000	Profit or loss	30,000
	30,000		30,000
20X8			
Tax Liability a/c (underprovision 20X7)	2,000	Profit or loss	42,000
Tax liability a/c	40,000		
	42,000		42,000

chapter 3

Tangible and intangible assets

- Overview.
- Measurement.
- Depreciation.
- Revaluations.
- IAS 38 Intangible Assets.
- IAS 36 Impairment of Assets.

Tangible and intangible assets

Overview

This chapter deals with the following standards that regulate the accounting for non-current assets:

- IAS 16 Property, Plant and Equipment.
- IAS 38 Intangible Assets, including research and development costs.
- IAS 36 Impairment.

CBA focus

Non-current assets are a key part of the standards for this unit. You are likely to be tested on them at some point in the exam.

Measurement

IAS 16 Property, Plant and Equipment provides guidance on non-current assets.

Key points:

- A non-current asset should be initially measured at its cost.
- Cost includes all costs that are directly attributable in bring the asset to its working condition for its intended use.
- Subsequent expenditure on an asset can be capitalised if it enhances the economic benefits of the asset, such as reconditioning an asset to provide additional years of use.

Depreciation

Definition

Depreciation represents the consumption of a non-current asset in the accounting period.

Non-current assets are used in the business to earn revenue. Charging depreciation means that the revenue earned is matched with the cost of using that asset. This applies the **accruals** concept.

The method of depreciation should be the one which gives the best estimate of the benefits of the asset consumed during the accounting period:

Benefits consumed equally in all periods	Benefits consumed more in earlier than later periods
↓	↓
Straight line	Diminishing balance

Example

A non-current asset costs £10,000, has a residual value of £2,000 and an estimated life of 4 years.

What is the annual depreciation charge using the straight line method?

Solution

$$\frac{\text{Original cost} - \text{residual value}}{\text{Estimated useful life}}$$

$$\frac{£10,000 - £2,000}{4 \text{ years}}$$

This gives a depreciation charge of £2,000 each year.

Revaluations

Key points:

- Revaluation of assets is permitted but not required. If revaluations take place all assets of the same class must be revalued.

- Companies may wish to revalue assets to show a more up to date value of the assets in the business.

- If the difference between the carrying amount and the revalued amount is a gain on revaluation, it is credited to a reserve in the statement of financial position called the revaluation surplus and disclosed in the statement of changes in equity.

- If there is a loss (decrease) on revaluation, it is recognised in the statement of profit or loss unless there is already a balance in the revaluation surplus relating to that asset. In that case, the decrease is first taken to the revaluation surplus with any remainder in the statement of profit or loss.

- Depreciation on a revalued asset is based on the revalued amount not the cost. If the asset has increased in value this will give a higher depreciation charge. The revalued asset is depreciated over its remaining useful life from the date of revaluation.

- The depreciation charge on the revalued asset will be different to the depreciation that would have been charged based on the previous asset value. As a result of this, a transfer should be made of an amount equal to the excess depreciation from the revaluation surplus to retained earnings. The double entry for this transfer is shown below:

Dr Revaluation surplus
Cr Retained earnings

The above transfer is only required if it is company policy to make a transfer in respect of excess depreciation on revalued assets. If this is not the case then a reserves transfer is not necessary.

Example

KL Ltd own buildings which cost £350,000 on 1 January 20X4. Depreciation is charged over 50 years. On 1 January 20X6, the buildings were revalued to £480,000.

Calculate the gain on revaluation and the carrying amount of the buildings at 31 December 20X6.

Solution

We will approach this question step by step as there are a number of stages to deal with.

1. Calculate the carrying amount at the date of revaluation

	£
Cost	350,000
Depreciation to 31/12/X5 350,000 ÷ 50 × 2 years	(14,000)
CA at 1/1/X6	336,000

2. Calculate the gain on revaluation

	£
Revalued amount	480,000
Less carrying amount	(336,000)
Gain on revaluation	144,000

DR Non-current assets – cost (480,000 – 350,000)	130,000
DR Accumulated depreciation	14,000
CR Revaluation surplus	144,000

3. Calculate the carrying amount at 31 December 31/12/X6

	£
Revalued amount	480,000
Depreciation to 31/12/X6 480,000 ÷ 48 years	(10,000)
CA at 31/12/X6	470,000

> Note that once the asset has been revalued, the depreciation is calculated for the remaining useful life, in this case – 48 years.

Example

KL Ltd's accounting policy is to make the annual transfer within the SOCIE to transfer the 'excess depreciation' from revaluation surplus to retained earnings.

Calculate the excess depreciation and show the journal entries required to transfer the excess depreciation from the revaluation surplus to retained earnings at 31/12/X6.

Solution

The transfer in the SOCIE is: £10,000 - £7,000 =	£3,000
Dr: Revaluation surplus	£3,000
Cr: Retained earnings	£3,000
CA of revaluation surplus at 31/12/X6 is £144,000 - £3,000 =	£141,000

IAS 38 Intangible Assets

Definition

IAS 38 Intangible Assets defines an intangible asset as **'an identifiable, non-monetary asset without physical substance.'** (IAS 38, para 8).

To be identified as an intangible asset, an asset must either:

- be capable of being separated or divided from the entity and sold, transferred, licensed, rented or exchanged either individually or together with a related contract, asset or liability; or
- arise from contractual or other legal rights.

Internally generated goodwill should not be recognised as an asset as it is not a separable asset, it doesn't arise from contractual rights and it cannot be measured reliably.

Recognition and measurement

- An intangible asset shall only be recognised if:
    - it is probable that the expected future economic benefits that are attributable to the asset will flow to the entity; and
    - the cost of the asset can be measured reliably.
- An intangible asset shall initially be measured at cost.

Research and development costs

An entity must distinguish between:

- the research phase
- the development phase.

Tangible and intangible assets

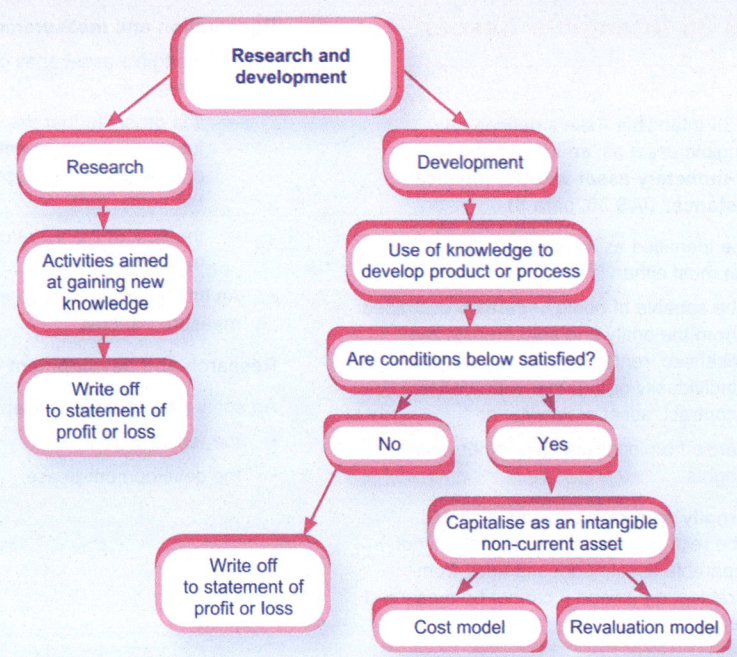

Expenditure on the **research** phase is recognised as an expense in the statement of profit or loss when it is incurred and cannot be recognised as an intangible asset.

Expenditure on the **development** phase can be recognised as an intangible asset providing the entity can demonstrate all the following conditions:

(a) technical feasibility of completing the intangible asset so it is available for use or sale.

(b) intention to complete the intangible asset and use or sell it.

(c) ability to use or sell the intangible asset.

(d) how the intangible asset will generate probable future economic benefits.

(e) availability of adequate technical, financial and other resources to complete the development and to use or sell the intangible asset.

(f) ability to measure reliably the expenditure attributable to the intangible asset during its development.

Internally generated brands, publishing titles, customer lists and similar items cannot be recognised as intangible assets.

Subsequent measurement

The cost model or revaluation model must be chosen to account for the asset once recognised.

- **Cost model:** The asset is carried at cost less any accumulated amortisation and any accumulated impairment losses.

- **Revaluation model:** The asset is carried at its revalued amount. This is its fair value at the date of revaluation less any subsequent accumulated amortisation and any subsequent impairment losses. The valuation must be reviewed regularly.

Tangible and intangible assets

Amortisation of an intangible asset

A company should assess the expected useful life of an intangible asset:

Finite

Amortise the asset over its useful life starting when the asset is available for use.

(Development expenditure is deemed to be available for use when commercial production of the product being developed begins.)

Amortisation should reflect the pattern of use of the asset.

Residual value is zero unless:
- a third party has agreed to buy the asset at the end of the useful life
- there is an active second-hand market which can be used to measure a residual value.

Indefinite

Do not amortise, instead test for impairment annually.

Review the useful life each accounting period. If the asset now has finite useful life, it should be amortised.

IAS 36 Impairment of Assets

Definition

Impairment is the reduction in the recoverable amount of a non-current asset below its carrying amount.

Recoverable amount is the higher of the fair value less costs to sell and value in use.

Fair value less costs to sell is the amount at which an asset could be disposed of, less any direct selling costs.

Value in use is the present value of the future cash flows arising from an asset's continued use, including those resulting from its ultimate disposal.

Indicators of impairment

The following are indicators that an asset may be impaired:

- a current period operating loss or net cash outflow from operating activities
- a significant decline in a non-current asset's market value during the period
- obsolescence or physical damage to a fixed asset
- a significant adverse change in the business or the market in which the fixed asset or goodwill is involved
- a management commitment to undertake a significant reorganisation
- a major loss of key employees, or
- a significant increase in market interest rates.

Recognising impairment losses

- Impairment losses are recognised in the statement of profit or loss, unless they arise on a previously revalued asset.
- Impairment losses on revalued assets are taken to the revaluation surplus for that asset with any remaining loss charged to the statement of profit or loss.

Tangible and intangible assets

- After recognition of the impairment loss the depreciation charge for the asset shall be adjusted to allocate the asset's revised carrying amount over its remaining useful economic life.

Example

P Ltd owns plant and machinery that cost £150,000 on 1 January 20X2. It is depreciated over 15 years and on 1 January 20X5 it was revalued to £180,000. On 1 January 20X7, the assets were impaired and were written down to £120,000.

Calculate the impairment loss and show where it will be recorded.

Solution

1 Calculate the carrying amount at the date of revaluation

	£
Cost	150,000
Depreciation to 31/12/X4	
150,000 ÷ 15 × 3 years	(30,000)
CA at 1/1/X5	120,000

2 Calculate the gain on revaluation (1/1/X5)

	£
Revalued amount	180,000
Less carrying amount	(120,000)
Gain on revaluation	60,000

DR Non-current assets – cost	
(180,000 – 150,000)	30,000
DR Accumulated depreciation	30,000
CR Revaluation surplus	60,000

3 Calculate the carrying amount at 31 December 20X6

	£
Revalued amount	180,000
Depreciation to 31/12/X6 180,000 ÷ 12 × 2 years	(30,000)
CA at 1/1/X7	150,000

4 Record the impairment on 1 January 20X7

	£
Revised value	120,000
Less CA	(150,000)
Impairment loss	30,000

As this is a revalued asset and there is sufficient revaluation surplus remaining, this impairment loss can be taken to the revaluation surplus rather than the statement of profit or loss.

DR Revaluation surplus	30,000
CR Accumulated depreciation	30,000

chapter 4

Key accounting standards

- Overview.
- IAS 2 Inventories.
- IFRS 16 Leases.
- IAS 10 Events after the Reporting Period.
- IAS 37 Provisions, Contingent Liabilities and Contingent Assets.
- Other accounting standards IFRS 15 Revenue from Contracts with Customers.

Overview

This chapter deals with the main points of accounting standards not dealt with in other chapters:

- A reminder of inventory valuation principles (IAS 2).
- The treatment of leased assets in accordance with (IFRS 16).
- The impact on financial statements of events which take place after the reporting period (IAS 10).
- The treatment of provisions and contingencies (IAS 37).

CBA focus

One or more of the topics covered in this chapter can be expected to appear in examination tasks.

IAS 2 Inventories

Key Point

- 'Inventories are required to be stated at the lower of cost and net realisable value.' (IAS 2, para 9).
- Cost includes all costs of purchase, conversion and other costs incurred in bringing the inventory to its present location and condition.
- Methods of costing identical items of inventory include:
  - **Unit cost** – the actual cost of purchasing or manufacturing inventory
  - **Weighted average cost** – calculating an average price for the inventory as it is purchased or sold.
  - **FIFO** (first in first out) – calculation that assumes the inventory held represents the latest purchases and the earlier purchases are included in sales.

IFRS 16 Leases

Definitions

A lease is a contract, or part of a contract, that conveys the rights to use an asset (the underlying asset) for a period of time in exchange for consideration' (IFRS 16, Appendix A).

A lessor is the entity that provides the right-of-use asset and, in exchange, receives consideration.

A lessee is the entity that obtains use of the right-of-use asset and, in exchange, transfers consideration.

A right-of-use asset represents the lessee's rights to use an underlying asset over the lease term.

Accounting for leases

Initial measurement

At the commencement of the lease, the lessee should recognise a lease liability and a right-of-use asset. The lease liability is initially measured at the present value of the lease payments that have not yet been paid. The discount rate should be the rate implicit in the lease. The right-of-use asset is initially recognised at cost, which comprises:

- The amount of the initial measurement of the lease liability

- Any lease payments made at or before the commencement date

- Any initial direct costs

- The estimated costs of removing or dismantling the underlying asset in accordance with the terms of the lease.

Key accounting standards

Subsequent measurement

Asset

The right-of-use asset is measured using the cost model (unless another measurement model is chosen). This means that it is measured at its initial cost less accumulated depreciation and impairment losses. The asset is depreciated over the shorter of the asset's useful life and the lease term, unless ownership of the asset transfers to the lessee at the end of the lease, in which case depreciation should be charged over the asset's useful life.

Liability

The liability is measured using amortised cost, which is the initial value plus any interest charged minus any payments made.

Example

A lessee enters into a lease on 1 January 20X6 for an item of plant with a useful life of four years. The following details are relevant:

Useful life of the asset   4 years

Present value of lease payments
£25,000

Lease terms   £7,500 pa paid in advance for four years, the first rental payable on 1 Jan X6

Interest rate implicit in lease   13.7%

Calculate the interest charge and the closing obligation over the period of the lease.

Solution

The easiest way to deal with leases is to put the information in a table and work through year by year. That way you can calculate the interest and the obligation in the same working.

The interest column shows the interest charge for each year. Notice how it reduces as the obligation is reducing.

The balance c/fwd column shows the obligation for the lease at the end of each year. This represents the total amount still owed.

	Balance b/fwd	Payment	Amount borrowed	Interest 13.7%	Balance c/fwd
Year ended 31 Dec X6	25,000	(7,500)	17,500	2,398	19,898
Year ended 31 Dec X7	19,898	(7,500)	12,398	1,698	14,096
Year ended 31 Dec X8	14,096	(7,500)	6,596	904	7,500
Year ended 31 Dec X9	7,500	(7,500)	0		

Short life and low value assets

If the lease is short-term (less than 12 months at the inception date) or of a low value then a simplified treatment is allowed.

The lessee can choose to recognise the lease payments in profit or loss on a straight line basis. No lease liability or right-of-use asses would be recognised.

IAS 10 Events after the Reporting Period

Definitions

- Events after the reporting period are those events, **'favourable and unfavourable, that occur between the end of the reporting period and the date when the financial statements are authorised for issue.'** (IAS 10, para 3)
- **Adjusting events** are events after the reporting period that provide evidence of conditions that existed at the end of the reporting period.
- **Non-adjusting events** are events after the reporting period that are indicative of conditions that arose after the end of the reporting period.

Accounting treatment:

- **Adjusting events** affect the amounts stated in the financial statements so they must be **adjusted**.
- **Non-adjusting events** do not concern the position at the end of the reporting period so the financial statements are not adjusted. If the event is material then the nature and its financial effect must be **disclosed**.

Examples of adjusting events:

- The sale of inventory after the year-end date that gives evidence about the inventory's net realisable value at the end of the reporting period.
- The bankruptcy of a customer after the reporting period that confirms that an allowance is required against a receivable balance at the end of the reporting period.

- The discovery of fraud or errors that show that the financial statements are incorrect.
- The settlement after the reporting period of a court case that confirms that the entity had a present obligation at the end of the reporting period. This would require a provision to be recognised in the financial statements (or an existing provision to be adjusted).

Examples of non-adjusting events that would require disclosure:

- A major business combination after the reporting period or disposing of a major subsidiary.
- Announcing a plan to discontinue an operation.
- Major purchases and disposals of assets.
- Destruction of a major production plant by a fire after the reporting period.
- Announcing or commencing a major restructuring.
- Abnormally large changes after the end of the reporting period in asset prices or foreign exchange rates.

Dividends:

- Ordinary dividends declared **after** the reporting period are **not recognised** as liabilities at the statement of financial position.
- This is consistent with IAS 37 and the definition of a liability in the Framework.

Key accounting standards

IAS 37 Provisions, Contingent Liabilities and Contingent Assets

Definition (IAS 37, para 10)

- A **provision** is a liability of uncertain timing or amount.
- A **liability** is a present obligation arising from past events.
- An **obligating event** is an event that creates a legal or constructive obligation.
- **Constructive obligation** – this arises from an entity's past actions, where there is a pattern of past practice that indicates they will behave in a certain way e.g. remedy environmental damage even if not legally required.
- IAS 37 prohibits provisions for future **operating losses** – they are avoidable.

CBA focus

In an exam task, ask yourself if the expenditure can be avoided.

If it can, there is no obligation and the provision should not be recognised.

Chapter 4

```
                    Provisions
                   /         \
     Recognition              Measurement
```

Recognition

Recognise when:
- an entity has a present obligation (legal or constructive) as a result of a past event,
- it is probable that a transfer of economic benefits will be required to settle the obligation, and
- a reliable estimate can be made of the amount of the obligation.

Measurement

The amount recognised:
- as a provision should be the best estimate of the expenditure required to settle the present obligation at the statement of financial position date.
- Where the time value of money is material, the provision should be discounted to present value.

Contingent assets and liabilities

- A **contingent liability** is a possible obligation arising from past events whose existence will only be confirmed on the occurrence of uncertain future events outside of the entity's control.

- A **contingent asset** is a **possible** asset that arises from past events and whose existence will only be confirmed on the occurrence of uncertain future events outside of the entity's control.

Contingent liabilities should not be recognised. They should be **disclosed** unless the possibility of a transfer of economic benefits is remote.

Contingent assets should not be recognised. If the possibility of an inflow of economic benefits is **probable** they should be **disclosed**.

Other accounting standards
IFRS 15 Revenue from Contracts with Customers

To recognise revenue in accordance with IFRS 15 an entity applies all of the following five steps:

- Step 1 – Identify the contract
- Step 2 – Identify the separate performance obligations within the contracts
- Step 3 – Determine the transaction price
- Step 4 – Allocate the transaction price to the performance obligations in the contract
- Step 5 – Recognise revenue when (or as) a performance obligation is satisfied

IFRS 15 says that 'revenue is recognised as control is passed, either over time or at a point in time.' [IFRS 15: 32]

If an obligation is satisfied at a point in time, recognise revenue at point the obligation is satisfied. This is likely to apply to the sale of goods.

If an obligation is satisfied over a period of time, recognise revenue over period of time that the obligation is satisfied. This is likely to apply to the provision of services.

If necessary, identify separate performance obligations and recognise revenue as each obligation is satisfied.

IAS 12 Income Taxes

- The tax charge in the statement of profit or loss comprises of the:
  - tax expense on profits for the period.
  - under/overprovision for previous year.

- Disclosure
  - The tax charge must be shown on the face of the statement of profit or loss.

Key accounting standards

chapter 5

Interpretation of financial statements

- Overview.
- Uses of ratios.
- Key ratios.
- Limitations of ratio analysis.

Interpretation of financial statements

Overview

This chapter deals with the topics involved in 'interpretation of accounts'. This includes:

- the uses of accounting ratios.
- the calculation and meaning of accounting ratios.
- the limitations of ratio analysis.

Uses of ratios

Key Point

- Ratio analysis is a means of interpreting financial statements.
- Users will review the financial statements and make decisions based on the information given. Ratios are calculated and compared with:
  - the performance of the business in previous years
  - the budgeted or planned performance in the current year
  - the performance of similar businesses.
- Ratios can assist in pointing the user of the financial statements to areas where the company may be performing particularly well or badly. They do not in themselves provide an answer but they can help in indicating the right direction for further investigation.

- The types of ratio to use will depend on the user of the information. For example, banks and lenders will be interested in liquidity ratios; management will be interested in profitability ratios.
- Ratios fall into several categories:
  - profitability ratios
  - liquidity and working capital ratios
  - investor ratios.

Key ratios

CBA focus

Ratios are important tools to assist in the interpretation of financial statements. You must learn these ratios and be able to calculate and interpret them as an exam task will require you to do both.

Profitability ratios

- **Return on capital employed (ROCE) =**

$$\frac{\text{Profit from operations}}{\text{Capital employed}} \times 100$$

Capital employed = equity + non-current liabilities

ROCE is very important as it shows the profit generated from the capital employed in the business. If ROCE has increased it is due to either increases in profitability and/or increases in asset utilisation.

- **Return on shareholder's funds =**

$$\frac{\text{Profit after tax}}{\text{Total equity}} \times 100$$

- **Gross profit percentage =**

$$\frac{\text{Gross profit}}{\text{Revenue}} \times 100$$

This shows the profit made on revenue before accounting for overhead costs. An increase or decrease may be due to a change in the sales mix, changes in costs or selling prices.

- **Expense/Revenue percentage**

$$\frac{\text{Specified expense}}{\text{Revenue}} \times 100$$

This can apply to any expense

- **Operating profit percentage =**

$$\frac{\text{Operating profit}}{\text{Revenue}} \times 100$$

This shows the profitability after taking into account expenses. A change may be due to changes in costs. You might expect an increase if sales have increased, but must watch out for costs that are rising above any sales increase as it may be that costs are not being controlled.

Liquidity

- **The current ratio =**

$$\frac{\text{Current assets}}{\text{Current liabilities}}$$

- **The quick ratio =**

$$\frac{\text{Current assets} - \text{inventory}}{\text{Current liabilities}}$$

These two ratios show whether a business can cover its current liabilities from current assets. The quick ratio removes inventory as this is the least liquid current asset. If the ratio is too low, it may suggest the business will have trouble paying current liabilities and if the ratio is too high it may suggest that working capital is not being used efficiently.

This ratio can vary greatly from industry to industry.

Use of resources

- **Inventory turnover =**
  $$\frac{\text{Cost of sales}}{\text{Inventories}}$$

  Companies have to strike a balance between being able to satisfy customers' requirements from inventory and the cost of having too much capital tied up in inventory.

- **Inventory holding period =**
  $$\frac{\text{Inventories}}{\text{Cost of sales}} \times 365 \text{ days}$$

  This shows how long inventory is being held before use.

- **Asset turnover (net assets) =**
  $$\frac{\text{Revenue}}{\text{Total assets - current liabilities}}$$

- **Trade receivables collection period =**
  $$\frac{\text{Trade receivables}}{\text{Revenue}} \times 365 \text{ days}$$

  If the receivables collection period becomes too high, the business may suffer from poor cash flow. Retail companies do not usually have receivables so this ratio would be irrelevant for those companies.

- **Trade payables payment period =**
  $$\frac{\text{Trade payables}}{\text{Cost of sales}} \times 365 \text{ days}$$

  Extending the payables payment period can be a cheap source of finance but companies run the risk of upsetting suppliers and not being offered credit in the future.

- **Working Capital Cycle =**
  Inventory days + Receivables days – Payables days.

- **Asset turnover (non-current assets) =**
  $$\frac{\text{Revenue}}{\text{Non-current assets}}$$

Interpretation of financial statements

Financial position

- **Interest cover =**

  $$\frac{\text{Operating profit}}{\text{Finance costs}}$$

  This shows how many times the interest charge can be paid out of the current profits. It is a measure of security - the higher the ratio, the more secure the interest payment.

- **Gearing =**

  $$\frac{\text{Non-current liabilities}}{\text{Total equity + Non-current liabilities}} \times 100$$

  This ratio shows the proportion of debt to total finance in the business (equity plus debt). The higher the gearing ratio, the riskier a company is seen to be as debt interest must be paid out before dividends.

Limitations of ratio analysis

- Ratios do not provide answers; they merely highlight significant features or trends in the financial statements. They usually highlight areas that need further investigation.
- Be mindful of seasonal trade as accounting year-ends are often just after the seasonal trend is over when the business is at its best.
- Watch out for window dressing in the financial statements such as collecting receivables just before the year-end in order to show a larger cash balance and lower receivables than is normal.
- Accounting ratios are based on accounting information and are only as accurate as that underlying accounting information.
- If comparisons are to be made they must be with companies with a similar trade, otherwise the pattern of ratios will be different and the comparisons meaningless.

chapter 6

Statement of cash flows

- Overview.
- Preparing a statement of cash flows.
- Interpretation of a statement of cash flows.

Statement of cash flows

Overview

This chapter deals with:

- The purpose of a statement of cash flows and the information which it provides in addition to that contained in the statement of financial position and statement of profit or loss.
- The suggested format of a statement of cash flows in accordance with IAS 7 is presented and explained.
- The technique for the preparation of a statement of cash flows in an examination is illustrated.
- The points to look for when interpreting a statement of cash flows are outlined.

CBA focus

It is very likely that part of a task in your examination may involve the preparation of a statement of cash flows.

- A statement of cash flows can provide information on a company's liquidity, viability and adaptability.
- It may assist users of financial statements in making judgements on the amount, timing and degree of certainty of future cash flows.
- It gives an indication of the relationship between profitability and cash generating ability, and thus of the quality of the profit earned.

CBA focus

The examination may divide the statement into two parts.

- 'Profit before tax' to 'Net cash from operating activities'; and
- 'Net cash from operating activities' to 'cash and cash equivalents at the end of period'.

IAS 7 Statement of Cash Flows does not prescribe a strict format for the statement of cash flow, but it requires that it is split into three sections – operating, investing and financing.

XYZ Ltd, Statement of cash flows for the year ended 31 December 20X7

	£000	£000
Cash flows from operating activities		
Profit before tax	X	
Adjustments for:		
Depreciation charges	X	
Loss/(Profit) on sale of non-current asset	X/(X)	
Finance costs	X	
Investment income	(X)	
	X	
(Increase)/decrease in inventories	(X)/X	
(Increase)/decrease in trade and other receivables	(X)/X	
Increase/(decrease) in trade payables	X/(X)	
Cash generated from operations	X	
Interest paid	(X)	
Tax paid	(X)	
Net cash from operating activities		X
Cash flows from investing activities		
Cash paid to purchase property, plant and equipment	(X)	
Cash proceeds from sale of PPE	X	
Interest received	X	
Dividends received	X	
Net cash used in investing activities		(X)
Cash flows from financing activities		
Proceeds from issue of shares	X	
Redemption of long term borrowing	(X)	
Dividends paid	(X)	
Net cash used in financing activities		(X)
Net increase in cash and cash equivalents		X
Cash and cash equivalents at beginning of period		X
Cash and cash equivalents at end of period		X

Statement of cash flows

For the purpose of this unit the reconciliation of profit or loss to the net cash from operating activities may begin with profit from operations. If this is the case then the finance costs and the investment income will not need to be adjusted for as shown in the above proforma.

Preparing a statement of cash flows

Process:

- insert the net increase or decrease in cash and cash equivalents first. This is the figure the cash flow totals to and is an easy figure to calculate. It is the difference between cash and overdraft balances and short-term investments from the prior year to the current year. You can then fill in the opening balance of cash and cash equivalents. Then move on to the rest of the cash flow.

- start with cash from operating activities – insert profit before tax and add back deprecation and finance costs.

- next, deal with the movements in working capital. It can be tricky to remember which way round these figures should go. The following table summarises the treatment:

	Increase	Decrease
Inventory	Outflow	Inflow
Receivables	Outflow	Inflow
Payables	Inflow	Outflow

- work your way down the rest of the cash flow dealing with the easier figures first, such as interest, dividends and tax paid and movements in borrowing.

- finally, deal with the more difficult areas (such as non-current assets and movements in share capital) where a working is required in order to find relevant cash flow figures.

Chapter 6

CBA focus

- Cash flows are straightforward to produce if you follow a step-by-step process.
- Make sure you practise lots of questions so you are well prepared.
- Always aim to get the easy marks first and then go back and try the harder parts of the questions.

Example

The opening carrying amount of non-current assets is £490,580 and the closing balance is £567,210.

The depreciation charge for the year was £35,000.

There were disposals with a carrying amount of £43,000.

What is the cash paid for additions?

Solution

All the amounts need to be entered into the ledger account and then the missing figure is the balancing figure – in this case additions. This style of working can also be used to find tax paid.

Statement of cash flows

Non-current assets (CA)			
	£		£
Balance b/d	490,580	Depreciation	35,000
		Disposals	43,000
		Balance c/d	567,210
Cash additions (bal fig)	154,630		
	645,210		645,210

OR alternative working

Opening PPE	490,580
Depreciation	(35,000)
Disposals	(43,000)
Closing PPE	(567,210)
Purchase of PPE	**154,630**

Example

The following extract from the statement of financial position shows share capital and share premium:

	20X7	20X6
Capital and reserves	£	£
Share capital	135,000	120,000
Share premium	96,000	79,000

Calculate the cash received from the issue of shares.

Solution

If there has been a share issue in the year, we must remember to look at share premium as well as share capital as it is likely that the shares have been issued at a premium.

The movement is:

Increase in share capital (135,000 – 120,000)	15,000
Increase in share premium (96,000 – 79,000)	17,000
Total cash received from share issue	32,000

Example

The opening tax payable is £6,000 and the closing tax payable is £8,000. The charge in the statement of profit or loss is £7,000 for the year.

What is the cash paid in respect of tax?

Solution:

Tax payable

	£		£
Cash paid (bal fig)	**5,000**	Balance b/d	6,000
Balance c/d	8,000	Tax expense	7,000
	13,000		13,000

Once all the known amounts relating to tax are entered into the ledger account, the cash paid becomes the balancing figure.

Interpretation of a statement of cash flows

Things to look for

- Operating cash flow reflects how well a business is generating cash from its day to day activities. A negative operating cash flow is not good and suggests that the business is not operating efficiently. Also look at the effect on cash flow from working capital – inventories, receivables and payables.

- Good management of working capital can mean the business uses its cash effectively. Review the cash position as well as inventory levels, receivables and payables. For example, if inventory levels have risen, is it because of increased sales or could it be obsolete inventory? Does the company have the cash to pay for an inventory increase?

- If a company has made an investment in non-current assets, then they are obviously planning for the future which is a positive move. Comment on how they have financed this investment – by finance, cash, or share issues.

- If the company has no cash, sales of non-current assets may be a 'desperate' measure to raise cash.

- Review share issues and debt movements. Often this will correlate with non-current asset purchases so you can match the asset and its related finance.

- If the company is paying a dividend, look to see if there is sufficient cash to pay it. Many companies are reluctant to reduce the dividend as it sends a negative sign to shareholders.

chapter 7

Group accounts: basic principles and consolidated statement of financial position

- Overview.
- Consolidated statement of financial position.

Group accounts: basic principles and consolidated statement of financial position

Overview

This chapter will:

- Summarise the concept of a group and the process of consolidation.
- Set out tests of control in accordance with IFRS 10.
- Summarise and illustrate the three key workings normally needed to prepare a consolidated statement of financial position in an examination task.

CBA focus

- You can expect to see a group accounting question on this paper – either a statement of financial position or statement of profit or loss.
- You must have a logical approach to consolidations by using the workings below.

Key points

- A group consists of a parent company and subsidiary companies that are controlled by the parent.
- Consolidated financial statements combine the results and net assets of the parent and subsidiaries to show the group as a single entity.
- The performance of the group as a whole is shown in the consolidated financial statements.

Control

- When a parent acquires a subsidiary it is deemed to control that subsidiary when more than 50% of the ordinary share capital has been acquired.

- IFRS 3 defines a business combination as the bringing together of separate entities (i.e. companies) into one reporting entity. In most cases, when this occurs, one entity (the parent or acquirer) acquires control of the other entities (subsidiaries or acquirees). There are different ways a business combination can be effected. In the examples in this chapter and the next chapter, one company purchases the majority of shares in another company.

- IFRS 10 allows for situations where a parent doesn't own more than 50% of share capital but exercises control in some other way. In this case, the parent should consolidate the other company as a subsidiary regardless of the % shareholding.

- Per IFRS 10, an investor controls an investee if they have power over the investee, exposure to variable returns from its involvement with the investee, and the ability to use its power over the investee to affect the amount of the investor's returns.

Consolidated statement of financial position

There are 3 workings for the group statement of financial position. Working through these in an exam question provides you with a logical process towards completing the question.

Set out your workings as follows:

Group structure

The percentage will be given in the exam question.

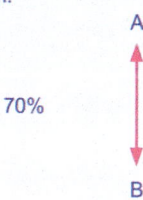

Group accounts: basic principles and consolidated statement of financial position

W1 Goodwill

Cost of investment	X
less: % of share capital acquired	(X)
% of retained earnings acquired	(X)
% fair value adjustments	(X)
Goodwill	X
Impairments	(X)
Goodwill in SFP	X

W1 Goodwill (alternative working)

Cost of investment	X
add: Non-controlling interest	X
less: Net assets of subsidiary at acquisition	(X)
Goodwill	X
Impairments	(X)
Goodwill in SFP	X

W2 Non-controlling interest

NCI % share capital	X
NCI % retained earnings	X
NCI % fair value adjustment	X
NCI	X

W3 Group retained earnings

Parent (100%)	X
Subsidiary	X
(Group share of post acquisition profit)	
Impairment	(X)
	X

Further points

- To calculate goodwill, you may need to adjust the subsidiary's assets at acquisition to their fair value.

- All companies in the same group should follow the same accounting policies.
- If there are any other reserves such as revaluation surpluses, they are treated in exactly the same way as retained earnings by taking the group share of the post acquisition movement on that reserve.

CBA focus

The process to follow is:

- Read the question.
- Start with the 3 workings and insert those figures into the answer.
- Add together the assets and liabilities of parent and subsidiary line by line to finish.

Example

J Ltd purchased 60% of the shares of R Ltd for £35,000 on 1 January 20X7. The retained earnings of R Ltd at that date were £14,000 and the non-current assets had a fair value of £6,000 more than their carrying amount at that date.

The statements of financial position as at 31 December 20X7 are below.

	J Ltd £000	R Ltd £000
ASSETS		
Non-current assets	20	22
Investment in R Ltd	35	–
Current assets	18	14
Total assets	73	36
EQUITY AND LIABILITIES		
Share capital (£1 shares)	20	10
Retained earnings	39	19
Current liabilities	14	7
Total equity and liabilities	73	36

Prepare the consolidated statement of financial position at 31 December 20X7.

Solution

Group structure

J

60%

R

(W1) Goodwill	£000
Cost of investment	35
Share capital acquired (10,000 × 60%)	(6)
Retained earnings acquired (14,000 × 60%)	(8.4)
Fair value adjustments (6,000 × 60%)	(3.6)
Goodwill in SFP	17

(W1) Goodwill (alternative presentation)	£000
Cost of investment	35
Non-controlling interest 40% × (10 + 14 + 6)	12
Net assets of subsidiary at acquisition 10 + 14 + 6	(30)
Goodwill in SFP	17

(W2) Non-controlling interest	£000
Share capital (10,000 x 40%)	4
Retained earnings at reporting date (19,000 x 40%)	7.6
Fair value adjustment (6,000 x 40%)	2.4
	14

(W3) Group retained earnings	£000
Parent company (100%)	39
Subsidiary: Group share of post acquisition profit (60% x (19-14)	3
	42

J Ltd, consolidated statement of financial position as at 31 December 20X7

ASSETS	£000
Non-current assets	
Goodwill (W1)	17
Property, plant and equipment (20 + 22 + 6)	48
Current assets (18 + 14)	32
Total assets	97
EQUITY AND LIABILITIES	
Share capital	20
Retained earnings (W3)	42
	62
Non-controlling interest (W2)	14
Current liabilities (14 + 7)	21
Total equity and liabilities	97

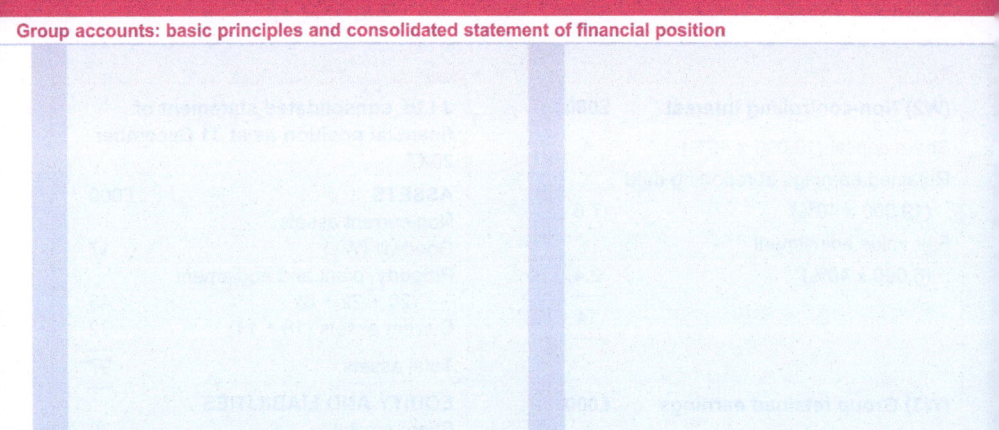

chapter 8

Group accounts: consolidated statement of profit or loss

- Overview.
- Consolidated statement of profit or loss.
- IFRS 10 Consolidated Financial Statements.

Overview

This chapter will:

- Show how to prepare a consolidated statement of profit or loss, based on the same principles as those underlying a consolidated statement of financial position.
- Summarise the main points of IFRS 10 on the regulation of consolidated financial statements.

CBA focus

- As with the statement of financial position, you must have a logical approach to consolidations by using the workings below.

Key points

- The consolidated statement of profit or loss shows the group as a single entity by combining the results of the parent and subsidiaries.
- Add together the results from revenue down to and including profit after tax to show the results of the group.
- Intra-group sales and purchases between the parent and subsidiary must be removed as the statement of profit or loss shows the transactions the group as a whole has made.
- Any dividends or interest paid to the parent from the subsidiary must be excluded from the group statement of profit or loss.

Chapter 8

Consolidated statement of profit or loss

Workings:

Group structure

The percentage will be given in the exam.

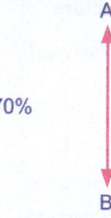

W2 Revenue and cost of sales

Don't forget to remove intercompany trading from revenue and cost of sales. The whole amount of sales or purchases between the group companies must be removed.

CBA focus

When dealing with inter company trading, it is important to remove THE SAME AMOUNT from both sales and from cost of sales. Failure to do this is a fundamental error of principle.

W3 Non-controlling interest

NCI share of subsidiary profit after tax   X

Example

Set out below are the draft statement of profit or loss of Perry Ltd and its subsidiary company Shale Ltd for the year ended 31 December 20X7.

On 31 December 20X5 Perry Ltd purchased 75% of the ordinary shares and 50% of the debentures of Shale Ltd. The issued share capital of Shale Ltd is 200,000 £1 ordinary shares, and it had £50,000 10% debentures outstanding on 31 December 20X7.

Shale Ltd pays its debenture interest on 31 December each year.

	Perry Ltd £	Shale Ltd £
Revenue	943,000	368,000
Cost of sales	(687,000)	(287,000)
Gross profit	256,000	81,000
Distribution costs	(76,000)	(26,000)
Admin expenses	(63,000)	(22,000)
Interest receivable – from group companies	2,500	–
Finance costs	–	(5,000)
Profit before taxation	119,500	28,000
Tax	(42,500)	(8,000)
Profit after taxation	77,000	20,000

During the year Perry Ltd sold goods to Shale Ltd for £112,000, making a profit of £35,000. These goods were all sold by Shale Ltd before the end of the year.

Prepare the consolidated statement of profit or loss for the year ended 31 December 20X7.

Solution

(W1) Group structure

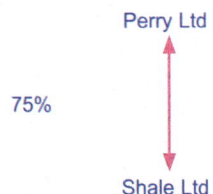

(W2) Revenue and cost of sales

The total revenue is £1,311,000 but the intra-group sales of £112,000 has been included as part of Perry Ltd's revenue and must be excluded, leaving £1,199,000.

Similarly, total cost of sales is £974,000 but the intra-group purchase of £112,000 has been included in cost of sales for Shale Ltd. It must be excluded, leaving £862,000.

(W3) Interest receivable

Interest receivable from group companies of £2,500 is Perry Ltd's share of the debenture interest. It must be cancelled against the finance cost in Shale Ltd to leave the net finance cost outside of the group of £2,500 (£5,000 – £2,500).

(W4) Non-controlling interests

The non-controlling interest is 25% of Shale Ltd's profit after tax figure = 25% × £20,000 = £5,000.

Perry Ltd, consolidated statement of profit or loss for the year ended 31 December 20X7

	£
Revenue (W2)	1,199,000
Cost of sales (W2)	(862,000)
Gross profit	337,000
Distribution costs (76,000 + 26,000)	(102,000)
Administrative expenses (63,000 + 22,000)	(85,000)
Finance costs (W3)	(2,500)
Profit before taxation	147,500
Tax (42,500 + 8,000)	(50,500)
Profit for the period	97,000
Attributable to:	
Equity holders of the parent	92,000
Non-controlling interests (W4)	5,000
	97,000

IFRS 10 Consolidated Financial Statements

Key points

- A company must prepare group financial statements if it is a parent company at its year-end (i.e. it has one or more subsidiaries). The consolidated financial statements must include all of the subsidiaries of the parent.

- IFRS 10 details the consolidation procedures that we have already seen in the previous chapters, such as the requirement to eliminate inter company trading.

- IFRS 10 also states that uniform accounting policies should be used for amounts included in the group financial statements.

References

References

The Board (2020) *Conceptual Framework for Financial Reporting.* London: IFRS Foundation.

The Board (2020) *IAS 1 Presentation of Financial Statements.* London: IFRS Foundation.

The Board (2020) *IAS 2 Inventories.* London: IFRS Foundation.

The Board (2020) *IAS 7 Statement of Cash Flows.* London: IFRS Foundation.

The Board (2020) *IAS 10 Events after the Reporting Period.* London: IFRS Foundation.

The Board (2020) *IAS 12 Income Taxes.* London: IFRS Foundation.

The Board (2020) *IAS 16 Property, Plant and Equipment.* London: IFRS Foundation.

The Board (2020) *IAS 36 Impairment of Assets.* London: IFRS Foundation.

The Board (2020) *IAS 37 Provisions, Contingent Liabilities and Contingent Assets.* London: IFRS Foundation.

The Board (2020) *IAS 38 Intangible Assets.* London: IFRS Foundation.

The Board (2020) *IFRS 3 Business Combinations.* London: IFRS Foundation.

The Board (2020) *IFRS 10 Consolidated Financial Statements.* London: IFRS Foundation.

The Board (2020) *IFRS 15 Revenue from Contracts with Customers.*

The Board (2020) *IFRS 16 Leases.* London: IFRS Foundation.

Index

Index

A

Accruals 10
Adjusting events 50
Asset 9

C

Charities 11
Constructive obligation 52
Contingent asset 53
Contingent liabilities 53

E

Elements of the financial statements 9
Equity 9
Expense/Revenue percentage 60
Expenses 9

F

Formats 18

G

Going concern 10
Gross profit percentage 59

I

IAS 1 Presentation of Financial Statements 5, 10
IAS 2 Inventories 46
IAS 7 Statement of Cash Flows 65
IAS 12 Income Taxes 55
IAS 16 Property, Plant and Equipment 32
IAS 33 Earnings per share 55
IAS 36 Impairment 32
IAS 37 Provisions, Contingent Liabilities and Contingent Assets 52
IFRS 3 73
IFRS 10 Consolidated Financial Statements 73, 84
IFRS 15 Revenue from Contracts with Customers 54
IFRS 16 Leases 47
Impairment of assets 41
Income 9

Index

International Accounting Standards Committee Foundation (IASCF) 6
Inventory holding period 61
Inventory turnover 61

L

Legal framework 7
Liability 9
Limited companies 11
Limited liability partnerships (LLPs) 11

N

Non-adjusting events 50
Not-for-profit organisations 11

O

Operating profit percentage 60

P

Partnerships 11
Provision 52
Public sector organisations 11

R

Ratios 58
Recoverable amount 41
Return on capital employed (ROCE) 59
Return on equity (ROE) 59

S

Sole traders 11
Statement of Cash Flows 63
Statement of Changes in Equity 23
Statement of financial position 19

T

The current ratio 60
The Framework for Financial Reporting 8
The quick ratio 60
Trade payables payment period 61
Trade receivables collection period 61

W

Working Capital Cycle 61

Index